# Way Station

*To Nancy –*
*a fantastic poet*
*and person –*
*Love, Leaie*

*poems by*

# Liane Ellison Norman

*Finishing Line Press*
Georgetown, Kentucky

# Way Station

ACKNOWLEDGMENTS

"Weighted," in a different version and with the title, "What There'd Been," won the
Wisteria Prize from Paper Journey Press in 2006.
"Bridges of Pittsburgh" and "Navigating Pittsburgh" appeared in *Pittsburgh City Paper* in
2011 and 2013 respectively.
"Self-Interest" will appear in Voices From the *Attic*, XVIV, an anthology published
annually by the Madwomen in the Attic of Carlow University.
"In the Interest of Public Health" appeared in the *Pittsburgh Post Gazette*, April 20, 2013.
Reprinted in *Verse Envisioned; Poems From the Post-Gazette* and *Works of Art They Have
Inspired,* Word Association Publishers, 2016.
"Lately" appeared in *Speaking for my Self: Twelve Women Poets in their Seventies and
Eighties,*" Ed. Sondra Zeidenstein, Chicory Blue Press, 2014.
"Black Man Walking" appeared in *Pittsburgh City Paper*, October 10, 2015.

Profound thanks to Jan Beatty, one of the world's wonders, for her wisdom and her eagle
eye. Also to Lisa Alexander, Tess Barry, Daniella Buccelli and Lori Wilson for careful
reading, good suggestions and unstinting support. Susan Sailor and Emily Mohn-Slate have
helped me think through—and re-think—a number of these poems. Celeste Gainey's kind
words and good advice have been invaluable: I am very grateful. My dear friend, Ruey
Brodine, provided the cover art. Thanks, too, to that extraordinary breed, the Madwomen
in the Attic, in both in its formal Carlow University and in its informal manifestations. In
the latter category, I am grateful to Jamie Benjamin, Rebecca Cole-Turner, Kay Comini,
Marilyn Marsh Noll, Joanne Samraney, M.A. Sinnhuber, and the late Lois Greenberg.

But above all, my gratitude to my husband, Robert T. Norman, for venturing into the foreign
country of poetry without a passport, but with endless good humor, energy and a sharp eye.

Publisher: Leah Maines
Editor: Christen Kincaid
Cover Art: Ruey Brodine
Author Photo: Marie Kamala Norman
Cover Design: Elizabeth Maines

Printed in the USA on acid-free paper.
Order online: www.finishinglinepress.com
              also available on amazon.com

Author inquiries and mail orders:
Finishing Line Press
P. O. Box 1626
Georgetown, Kentucky 40324
U. S. A.

# Table of Contents

# One

*The choice to speak*
*or not to speak.*
*We spoke.*
　　　　　*—Denise Levertov, Making Peace*

**2015**

In these latter days

    I throw my poems—

        small stones—into still ponds

In hope

    that someone

        will see rings.

**House of the World**

My husband went to Martin Luther King's March
on Washington, the rightful demand by Americans
of African descent, for full civil rights. Nine months
pregnant, I didn't want to give birth at the Reflecting Pool.

We took six-week-old Andy with us to stand outside
the Old Executive Office Building in gray November
to salute the murdered JFK who had fired us to do
good works in the larger world. With Andy, a year old,

to Kathmandu where my husband worked for USAID
and I finished my dissertation on George Eliot. Learned
the many-templed city before it was riddled with tourists.
Pregnant with Marie, we'd left Washington where the obstetrician

said, *You can't have a baby in Nepal. No one has babies in Nepal.*
But I gave birth to Marie in an old Rana palace in Kathmandu,
doctor just back from an elephant ride in the jungle called Terai.
Then to Kanpur, India, storied city on the Ganges,

where Bob organized an international seminar, I taught at IIT Kanpur.
Pregnant with Emily, moved to Pittsburgh where we both
taught and raised kids and took them with us to march Downtown
from the Hill, mourning the murdered Martin Luther King.

## Understory

The forest's canopy—tall trees above, understory below.
Those lower twigs wait, shoot up tall

when canopy trees die. In spring, before the canopy leafs out,
the understory gets full sunlight, only briefly,

but enough for a whole year's net carbon balance. The soil
beneath keeps cool and moist, provides fungi, microclimates

for small animals and plants, Tall, scrubby, big, little.
There's under, preposition showing relationship,

and story, narrative. When I was little I was told
*You're growing like a weed!*

Some thrive, some block the sun.

## Today They Discovered the God Particle
*—July 4, 2012*


Before I get to the *New York Times*
I stand on the front porch
for just the *idea* of cool air
on this already humid morning

while next door a backhoe drives off a jerry-rigged ramp from a truck
knocking loose the retaining wall
a former neighbor built with muscle and railway ties
The muddy machine rolls onto the lawn to dig a culvert
bulldozes spent peony bushes
piles up a mountain of red clay
to get at a sewer line blocked by pin oak roots

Across the street the first doe I've seen
in this neighborhood
on the lawn of the house
where the lesbian couple and three Chinese daughters live
Its slender neck stretches down
then alert    head up    ears fine-tuned
She stays there
long enough for me to admire her taut legs
then grazes away between houses

The backhoe leaves a rubble of upended grass, rocks, peonies
The doe vanishes
without so much as a hoof print

In the *New York Times* I find
that scientists think they have found the Higgs Boson particle
informally called God
what holds matter together

## Trees at the End of Winter

It still seems touch and go,
whether the trees, now bare
and elegant against a stormy sky,

will leaf again. Waking
this morning, I heard birds
through the window opened

just a crack for cool. Noticed
yesterday that tiny shoots
have pierced the sodden soil

of the garden, though snow's
predicted for tomorrow. I know
that soon the calligraphy

of bare Norway maple branches,
the two-year-old tulip poplar,
will conjure hints of green

and squirrels will race like
acrobats through all the trees
and we'll be reassured

that winter only lasts a season.

**Quiet Rooms**


The presidential candidate
said it was OK
to talk about income inequality
but only in *quiet rooms.*

Please tell me: where are
the *quiet rooms,* when
may we go into them
to discuss disparities,

who's rich? who isn't? why?
And who will lead
the conversation? How
will we consider

the kind of country
we want to be?

**Self-Portrait As I Am**


Not as I wish some Rembrandt
would set me down on canvas, illumined
by an inner radiance, flesh as fresh
as downy peach, eyes cast either down
or heavenward, maybe turned toward
an open window in hopes of revelation,
passer-by, friend, relation.

                         But nearly 80,
fleshier than I once was, some screws
coming loose, joint fatigue, falling face,

which the old Ogden photo shows fresh and curved,
birthmark re-touched out, long golden curls,
rosebud mouth, pale yellow dress,
blue ribbon threaded through eyelet.

Blood still courses in veins that stand
ropey and blue, little mountain ranges.

## Blue Bra

She was out in Cairo's
Tahrir Square
saying no
to the theft
of her future,
her blue bra
cupping
young breasts,
exposed
when soldiers
bludgeoned
her
for defending
hard-won
revolution,
ripped off
her concealing
abaya,
stomped
her slender
chest.
The bright
blue bra
shining out
went viral,
proclaimed
that under
the heavy layers
men hide
their women in,
an actual person
could make a choice
about—
if nothing else—
her underwear.

## Defenestration

Strong word: turn it with your tongue, in the gateway
of your teeth—the Defenestration of Prague—
political enemies thrown out windows.

*Fenetre*, say the French, *window*, opening to light,
to look out of. *Kings II* says Jezebel
was defenestrated by servants at the urging of Jehu

and English King John may have dropped his annoying
nephew from the window. An angry crowd defenestrated
patricians in Leuven and James II of Scotland tossed

the 8th Earl of Douglas out at Stirling Castle.
Lorenzo de' Medici defenestrated Jacopo de'Pazzi,
payback for conspiracy to murder. The stock market

crash led to defenestrations and girls
in the Triangle Shirtwaist factory jumped to their deaths
when their locked-up factory caught fire.

One man, to demonstrate how strong his office tower
windows were, accidentally defenestrated.
Office workers preferred defenestration to fire on 9/11.

## Tierra Rejada

The producers of *Chinatown* paid to film
a car chase in the orange orchard, shooters
firing blanks into the trees, on which—
among the real oranges—fake ones hung
with dynamite charges so it looked like bullets
hitting spitting juice. A car chase bashed
into a walnut tree, wrapped to protect the trunk.

~

My stepfather's ranch—citrus avocadoes walnuts,
little airstrip for his Cessna—the house
he brought my mother to after their spouses
each had died. Tierra Rejada, set in
dun and lavender hills of southern
California, rich green of watered crops.

~

The studio that made Lassie TV movies paid
to use land near the airstrip to make episodes.
One summer we watched, learned how
the wonder dog was really many collies
each with just one trick.

~

Faye Dunaway wanted my mother's
kitchen table chairs, graceful oak
around the cherry wood table that looked out
from an arch of white roses onto
acacia jacaranda walnuts. Mother said *No*.
Dunaway, used to getting her way
kept offering more: Mother stood firm.
My sister has the chairs. She says
the wood is drying, joints loosening.

## What I Didn't Expect—


that old is different from young—
the way you can't understand how atoms
juggle everything solid
or how the sun's hot plasma
is woven with hydrogen and helium—
that in the middle of the night
getting up to go to the bathroom
takes a moment's steadying—
that we still admire one another's aging bodies—
that my breasts sag, arms drape loose flesh—
that we lie in morning light, make love
to the sounds of birds, their separate lives,
the hush of snow—

## Punto in Aria

I was lonely and the project I had in mind wasn't working out.
I tried having the protagonist speak from beyond the grave. No good.
Perhaps a day in Berkeley. I could research 18th century birth control.

But first, breakfast at the Station House in Pt. Reyes Station,
eggs benedict and coffee, cooked and served by someone else.
Then the drive through dry gold hills, sun-shot forest
to San Rafael, across the Bay Bridge into Berkeley.

~

Walked past a map store, turned back. Might there be
maps of eighteenth-century Salzburg or Vienna?
No, just hiking maps of the Sierras. So I left.
The proprietor came running after me: she could order
what I wanted. At Bancroft Library I searched to find out
what an 18th century Salzburg woman might have used
for birth control after her sixth fragile child,
who had a malformed ear, second to survive infancy,
named Wolfgang Gottlieb
and we know as Wolfgang Amadeus Mozart.

~

In Bancroft Library I found a book about how women like her
tried—mostly in vain—to limit pregnancies.
So many babies:
so many deaths.

I didn't know enough to know
the world didn't need more words on Mozart,
but I'd already bought a volume of the Mozart family's letters.
In them discovered that Mozart had a mother.
Who knew?
Thought I'll write about *her*.
There were a few of her letters to and from her son, her husband.
Her portrait shows her holding a length of lace:
portraits of the time showed subjects with what they did.
Was she, maybe, a lacemaker? A length of lace, *punto in aria*,
lace was called in Italian,
stitches in air.

~

Then across campus to the music library where I found
Anna Pertl's family tree, her father, a court musician for a time.
Maybe I was right, that Mozart's *mother* was a composer
like her husband. Was that what Wolfgang's letter from Italy
to his mother, naming the mysterious Pertl Symphonies,
was about?

~

I drove back through San Rafael, sun-filtering forest,
dry hills, to the familiar cabin my husband and his father built
with their own hands, in which we were married on a clear June day,
sinking sun still sparking on Tomales Bay.

### Pith and Moment

*enterprises of great pith and moment*
*—Hamlet, Act III*

As I hang the first load of wash
on my new umbrella-folding clothesline
set in the 18-inch hole my son dug

among the hostas and spent spirea
in the back yard, where already cicadas
weave their late summer brocade,

I exult in the free sun and wind
lifting wet sheets and towels, socks,
underpants, shirts and jeans

that I fold down—dry—
into the laundry basket
at the end of a clear day.

**Perfect Mind**
*I fear I am not in my perfect mind.*
*—King Lear*

That centrifugal force of age,
being whirled towards a destination

of absence, of not existing, of never
having existed except as diminished

memory in others' minds. How odd
that Lear, his arrogance burned away,

his foolish judgments upended,
is wisest when his mind softens,

thaws, flows like water
and he knows his child.

## Way Station

*a place where people can stop for rest, supplies, etc. during
a long journey*
— Meriam Webster Dictionary

It's only just sinking in,
like water that has pooled
on the ground, too much

to be absorbed quickly—
what the gerontologist said,
*mild cognitive impairment,*

which seems to mean not yet
full-blown dementia but maybe
a way-station.

        I've grieved my father,
dead at 49, my daughter at 36, and now
grieve for the mind I once had,

dependable, clear, and—
I thought—not inclined
to walk out on a girl.

# Two

*Now when I look at my body*
*under the spell of gravity*
*I have to laugh*
        —Alicia Suskin Ostriker, "Our Dead Friend"

## A Field Book of the Stars


The flyleaf—*Harve, 1931,* my father's college friend
in his slanted script, *given to Lincoln Ellison.*
Below that, in Mother's hand, *Passed on to Liane and her family 1973.*
*We used to lie in our bedrolls and pick out the constellations.*


Here are accounts of Ursa Major, the great bear, who is also the big dipper;
Ursa Minor, little bear and dipper, whose handle passes through Polaris, the Pole
    Star.
The constellation Camelopardalis, the giraffe.
The stars of Gemini, the twins, seen by Arabs as a pair of peacocks,
by Egyptians as two sprouting plants,
Hindus as twin gods,
Buddhists as a woman holding a gold cord.


On Andromeda's page I read:
*The chief object of interest in this constellation is the great nebula.*
*It can be seen by the naked eye and is a fine sight in an opera glass.*
To identify planets: *If it is very red, it will probably be Mars.*
*Venus approaches nearer to the earth and is more brilliant than any other planet.*


My father loved to tell of the Norwegian sheepherder, Mormon convert,
who lay alone at night on the Wasatch Plateau above timber
freezing in his paltry blanket, scanning the stars for a sign
of salvation from Heaven. He found a starry formation he thought
was that sign: *CV. Vat it mean?* decided at last it meant, in his Norwegian English,
*Keep Vigglin'.* My father drew the story out with relish, kept
the punch line bobbing just out of reach as long as he could.


What the *Field Book* author couldn't imagine in 1907—
nor my parents—is that light from cities, highways,
my neighbor's left-into-February garland of outdoor Christmas bulbs,
would so often obscure any sign of stars—
ordinary stars, shooting stars, planets, meteors,
the night sky hazy.

## Surviving

One of the first things the people in Sarajevo did
after the mortars stopped coughing up death
was form a chamber orchestra. They needed
music to perfect the silence after so much murder.

In Haiti, a violinist, Juilliard-trained, played
in his mind all the violin concertos one by one.
Their difficulty and fierce loveliness kept him alive
as he lay trapped and injured with his dead wife
in the ruins of the music school they'd built in Port-au-Prince.

## Lately

I've been rehearsing
death—
the next big thing:

like choosing and blooming
at the right college; like finding
the only man I've loved

and lived with
more than half
a century;

like giving  body's
lodgment
to infinitesimal

strangers,
who blossomed
from blastocysts

to three
particular people.
The daily signs—

too-soon
fatigue,
ache of hoisting

bone and flesh
up stairs,
lacunae

where once the right
word bounded
forward

like a friendly dog
with a slightly
slimy ball.

**January 26, 2015**


Snow falling—late yesterday afternoon,
all night, steadily all day—still falling.

The three-year-old tulip poplar's edged
on every twig in white and the hemlocks in back

sag with the weight of snow—8 inches so far,
judging from what builds on the bird bath.

Swags of snow burden the neighbor's Norway maple
and the ones behind it on the parallel block.

And quiet, no sound of traffic passing,
no sound of cars starting up, no mail so far

and maybe not at all. It's like a Quaker
silence of worship, busy motors

of talk and motion stilled.

### I made the most beautiful pizza


crust part flour, part fine cornmeal,
yeast, water with a little honey raised
all the warm afternoon, then rolled out

the springy dough that pushed back
under my hands, spread caramelized
onions, on the crust like jam, barely

poached asparagus spears in a sunburst,
slivers of prosciutto for color and salt,
all sprinkled with parmesan. Mother

taught me pride in *women's work,*
the heft of dough, meals nutritious
and lovely. Oven pre-heated to 450

for 10 minutes—then lower heat for 20—
and I was moving too fast, rammed
the pan into the top of the stove,

propelling the whole pizza off
and onto the bottom of the oven
where it burned and smelled burned.

## That Clean Strong Voice

I hadn't remembered how uncluttered
her prose, the just-right word,
a woman telling a woman's tale.
New to grasslands. Plains. How it is
to be a stranger. Almost newborn
in the middle of a mysterious continent.

I felt special kinship to Willa Cather
because I'd gone to college on the plains.
And we'd had the chance to buy the house
Cather lived in during part of her decade
in Pittsburgh. I remember wondering
if we'd find handwritten pages behind
a radiator, tattered notes in an old closet
with fusty wallpaper. We bought another
house two blocks from where she'd lived.

My book club chose *My Antonia.*
I read it with new pleasure.
Untamed prairie. Nebraska. Red grass
that stretched beyond sight.
Settlers from Bohemia, twice foreigners,
new to a strange land, where everyone
was a kind of stranger. Desperate winters.
Loneliness. That clean strong voice.

## Dig

Imagine finding a man's whole skeleton.
Then discovering
the injured bones were once King Richard III,
dead since 1485!

You go to work to operate the steam shovel,
excavate a parking lot in Leicester
and uncover the hacked bones
of a despised king, the scoliosis
plus evidence of battle wounds
that re-open wounds and battles:
who gets the bones? where should they rest?
who's legitimate? who's not?

The bones left long ago in a Franciscan priory
fallen to disrepair since Henry VIII
(heir to Richard's killer one generation removed)
separated England's church from Rome, dissolved
the monasteries, seized their wealth.

Now new quarrels: cities of Leicester and York
both want the bones to separate tourists from their money.
Queen Elizabeth II doesn't want them in Westminster Abbey:
she is, after all, the consequence
of the line of succession laid down by Richard's killer.

Leicester in the midlands, where the Battle of Bosworth Field
was fought, where Shakespeare's wicked Richard cries,
*A horse, a horse, my kingdom for a horse!*
(and once, I've heard, during a performance,
a drunken audience member laughed,
at which the actor on the stage flung out,
*Make haste and saddle yonder braying ass!*)

York to the north also claims the bones—
Richard was of the House of York, contender
in the Wars of the Roses, civil and uncivil battle,
dynasties fighting, Lancastrians and Yorkists—
Henry Tudor winning out at Bosworth Field.

Richard and Henry were rival parts of the same royal line—
Plantagenet—different branches of one tree.

Was Richard III Shakespeare's crooked villain
who needed to be done away with?

Or a good king basely murdered by someone
who wanted the throne for himself
and slandered the monarch he'd unseated?

## My Philosopher Son

expected that
      when he
           turned four

he'd be able
      to tie
           his shoes,

but on his birthday he couldn't
      so decided
           he must still be three.

### Delhi to Kathmandu
*—after Sarah Browning*


Flying that last leg in, Delhi to Kathmandu
on a DC-3, no safe water to mix with powdered milk
for Andy, a year old, so he cried himself to sleep
as we circled over the emerald-as-Oz city.

Hindu temples, Buddhist stupas,
skinny men carrying twice-their-size loads
tethered to forehead tump lines,
a woman sitting out in the sun, limp sari,

recovering from childbirth, a baby
that could fit in her hand at her breast.
Kids playing in the street,
buffalo wandering.

We were white in a green USAID jeep.
Nepalis were various browns, some
looking Indian, some Tibetan. Andy's blue eyes
were enormous at passing elephants

and flower-painted *Public Transport* trucks
driven by turbaned Sikhs. The main means
of transport, though, was feet, and I walked up
to my husband's office, pregnant, and

women smiled, touched my swelling belly
and one was surprised—in English—
*Memsahib having baby in tummy? Like Nepali?*
It was Marie Kamala, born in cool January

in an old Rana palace,
who breathed the life of this city,
speaks Nepali, climbed the Himalayas—
adopted a Nepali son.

**Watching Wit**


A stage play: British actors tell the story of a professor
        who teaches the complex wit of metaphysical poetry.

She's diagnosed with terminal ovarian cancer. The doctors don't know
        how to cure or care but from the planet of the latest theory.

One young doc was once her student. His medical role
        is to pry open her privacy with his speculum.

I found myself in tears, then sobbing from deeps I'd hovered over,
        remembering in every atom, how my daughter—

violinist of the intricate Baroque—declined, then finally died
        from the cancer no doctor could outwit.

How one humiliation follows another follows another. Her body,
        the canvas on which physicians limn their curiosity.

Finally, exhausted by pain and mortality, she starts to slip away.
        An elderly colleague comes, curls up on the bed with her,

softly reads *The Runaway Bunny*, a children's story both
        professors would have scorned professionally.

The kindly nurse holds off resuscitation brigades
        so that, at last, the dying woman can die.

## Bach Double

On the radio, driving home from my poetry workshop,
I hear the Bach Double Concerto for Two Violins on the car radio.
I pay attention to red lights, students wearing black in the dark,
deep in their iPods, wandering nearly invisible into the street.

The announcer says *It's Ann Akiko Meyers playing*
*on each of her two multi-million dollar Strads—*
*the 1697Napoleon/Molitor and the 1730 Royal Spanish—*
parts recorded separately, mechanically overlaid.

A violinist friend tells me, *Double, triple concertos*
*are conversations. The extemporaneous quality, the dialogue,*
*is integral.* That night in the car, it wasn't two voices
I heard conversing, but the same one talking to itself.

## Satellite Dolphins


The dolphins catch
fish in their beaky

mouths as neatly
as fielders baseballs.

Four or five of them
swim together,

circle low in the water.
Replete, they swim off,

leaving a circle in mud
on the ocean floor

for satellite cameras to see.
Smart, strategic, efficient,

they have no need for nuclear
bombs, armies or campaign funds.

They churn bottom
sediment in a cloud,

confusing fish
who rise, jump.

### To Paris on Spring Break
*—for Maggie Patterson*


Chilly spring,
forsythia timidly in bloom,
daffodils brave in frilled bonnets.
Maggie and I flew non-stop

Pittsburgh to Paris. We had a deal
on airfare and the *pension* at the top of a street
jeweled in fresh flowers, Israeli blood oranges,
fish gleaming on ice, fragrant bread just out of ovens.
We ate still-warm croissants for breakfast
from the bakery down the street,
onion soup and *tarte tatin* for dinner
in the restaurant where Hemingway hung out.

We saw the church where Mozart's mother's buried,
small St. Cecilia chapel—the saint in charge of music—
honors her, seconds my guess that she was a musician.
All over Paris, though an ocean away from Pittsburgh,
forsythia bloomed *provisoire*,
daffodils wore bonnets with *panache*.

We found Caravaggio's *Death of the Virgin* in the Louvre.
She lies in a red dress, feet toward us
who stand in front of the picture. The grieving
Magdalan buries her head in her arms.
Apostles can't look. The dead Mary—the model's a prostitute—
is an actual woman with calloused feet
from walking barefoot. Her body's beginning
to bloat. She's really dead. There are no cherubs
to waft her to Heaven, no magic to stop decay,
a painting rejected as unfit by the parish that commissioned it.

## A Day in the Waiting Room
*—for Kay Comini*


The dermatologist cut out the cancer,
sent my friend,
un-stitched,
compression bandaged,
to the waiting room where
the immense fish tank with live anemones
and Technicolor fish
bubbled and soothed.

We waited, waited.
The cut-out cells grew in their medium.
The wound was clean.
The doctor called her back, stitched her up,
put on thick bandages
and sent her home to hurt and heal.

I drove.
She flinched at the potholes I tried to miss,
said she'd sleep,
try to dream away the day.

## Bridges of Pittsburgh

I brag that there are more here than any city
in the world. Smithfield St. Bridge, second oldest
steel bridge in the country, 16th St. Bridge,

sundials on the piers, bridge after bridge
across conjoined rivers, Monongahela,
Allegheny, flowing west into the wide Ohio.

But it's the little stone bridges over streams
in the parks that move me most, so many built
by the WPA, rough hands, strong backs, hefting
stone to span streams in that cool of leaves
lit green in summer, golden in fall, dry rivulets
in winter. I think too of the quick bridge

a cardinal sketches in air from the neighbor's maple
to the pin oak next door. Single span of gold
as the yellow warbler dives into my purple monarda.
The spider constructs bridges of silk in rose leaves
and ivy. Bindweed strings itself from twig to branch.
Bridges we engineer and build, one to another.

**Every Year**


although
it's happened
before

I'm astounded
as the small blades
cut through wet soil

then
as if by magic
everything's
in bloom

# Three

*There is a forest where the trees*
*have mouths and speak*
*to woodsmen when they come*
*with axes.*
                    *—Ilze Klavina Mueller*

## Why Middlemarch Made Me Cry

When the women soccer players, Japanese and American, in clean
team uniforms streamed onto German turf to play for the World Cup,
I surprised myself by weeping. These women from countries that once

bombed and burned their grandparents; women running flat out,
skidding on slick grass, injured, muddy, hair plastered against sweaty heads.
It was the pleasure of bodies—nothing dainty, pretty, nothing lady-like.

They were everything Mother told me would scare men away. I learned
from my father not to complain, to be the hardy son he wanted
but didn't get. When I was pregnant with my third child, Mother told me

if I let on I was smart, my marriage would wither.
But by then I'd discovered *Middlemarch*, which left me trembling.
As if lightning lighted up my organs. Because I knew Dorothea

from inside, smart, yearning for purpose, a way to mark the world for good.
She took me in, knew my core, the self-importance, doubt, the declaration
*I'm here in the world. What can I do?*

Dorothea has so little room to move: long Victorian skirts, bonnets to hedge
her vision. She wants to do good in the world. Real work. But has so few
avenues. The bustling town of Middlemarch doesn't want a strong,

smart woman to do anything, much less change the world. Eliot knew it.
Hated it. Taught me what I knew about myself but didn't know I knew.
I think of her generosity and weep, watch the soccer players stretch out

strong arms and legs, run, sweat, fall in the dirt, get up and hug one another.

## Weighted

After my daughter died, I woke
weighted, no, she wouldn't call *Hi, Ma,*
that day forever. My father would forever
never meet his sons-in-law nor grandchildren.

The city's not in flames, my house no craze
of fuming rubble, neighbors not ripped apart,
not shrieking. Even so the missing tooth
preoccupies the tongue.

## Tornado in Oklahoma

The TV interviewer said
      to the woman who stood
            framed in wreckage.

"I'll bet you thank God."
      "No," she said, "I don't
            believe in God."

If she had believed deity
      caused her survival,
            would she be saying,

that God had decided for her and
      against those homeless,
            dead and injured?

## I love the names of things

*Butterfly, bumblebee,*
*snowstorm*, all airborne.

*Worms* turn the soil,
*lavender* stains my hands

with fragrance, lingers
in drawers and closets.

*Columbine*, pink and purple,
wild in my Pittsburgh garden,

but in the Wasatch Mountains
it's a white so crystalline

it takes your breath. *Butter*,
churned and turned

into pats. *Cherries*
twinned by stems,

golden Queen Anne to ruby
Bing, from Persia to Rome.

When we picked them
from the long ladder,

we hung them in pairs
from our ears.

## Finding My Way in the Dark

My bladder calls me from the little
death of sleep and I swim up

out of that depth, roll onto my
sore right hip, stand for seconds

testing for balance. I'm blinded
by blacker air that laps me,

bare feet gripping the hard bristle
of carpet. I touch the footboard knob,

tracing along the wooden curve
to the darker dark of doorway.

Finger along the hall molding
to the bathroom, icy tile even

in summer, toilet under the window
barely lit from the street. I pee, flush,

can now see in blackness small spasms
and splices of light, hear pre-dawn

calligraphy of birds. Make my naked way
back into bed against the firm,

warm body beside me, ride
the brief slide back down to sleep.

## Treachery


of ice, mimic of moisture.
But how did I get off the sidewalk,
landing headfirst in the street?
Left arm shooting fire and shock,
street too slippery for cars,
body too cumbered for will or legs.
Somehow scrambled up,
left side pure bruise,
hurt in joint and bone,
edged back toward home.

## Headlong

Rushing
towards the end
of everything,

the way
the Great Plains
have baked
and blackened

drying out
each
thread of silk
so that it can't

catch the pollen
that fertilizes
every single
kernel
of corn.

The care nature
takes, making
an ear
that can't hear

but answers need.

The long crack
near the tip
of Greenland's
Petermann Glacier,

the part sticking out
in the water,
what climate scientists
call a *frozen tongue*

has broken free,
*calved*,
an iceberg 46
miles square.

These breaks
don't *prove*
but alarm
the scientists

who are not
divided

about what's
causing
drought in Iowa,

hurricane
along
the Eastern Seaboard.

The earth
we once called
Mother.

## The Trumpeter of Krakow

The sentinel standing
atop St. Mary's church tower
in Krakow, blew the natural trumpet,
tones shaped by his lips,
to signal the daily opening, closing
of city gates, fire, sighting of Mongols
alerting the townsfolk.
In 1241, a Tatar arrow straight
through his throat stopped him.
All these centuries later
that same alarm—
cut short at the same place—
sounds every day
from the tower.

## Interior with Red Oak Coffee Table

Vermeer's light through windows,
      the clear afternoon sunshine cooled

by the only original front porch left
      on the block, filtered through old lace

curtains to fall on the new table
      just up from my husband's workshop.

This is home. We don't often see it
      because we live here and don't often look.

## Self-Interest

The world I live in
doesn't need God,
not to make it go

not to save it.
We just look around
and say: here's

where I live;
I won't foul my nest,
which is your nest, too.

## Snow Blind

We were driving back in wind, half-hearted flakes,
Morgantown to Pittsburgh. It was dark,
light rain mixed with half-hearted snow,
headlights reflecting off night air.
At the Pittsburgh exit, sudden theatrics of sky—
Wagnerian lightning—each flash a sheet
across the universe, thunder like battalions
of kettle drums, thick swirl of blindness.
Cars crawled onto the parkway like patients
recovering from surgery, afraid to touch
or bump the furniture.

## Navigating Pittsburgh

Odd turns take you by surprise—
across a river you hadn't meant to cross,
streets that don't run parallel, but a street
that parallels itself, hills, hollers,
confounding all sense of direction,
the way people tell you *turn right*
*where the Gulf station used to be.*

Today's quick trip down to the Strip,
miraculous parking space
in front of Pennsylvania Macaroni,
cheese from all over the world,
fresh bread, olives shimmering
in buckets of oil, handmade pasta.

Across the Allegheny on the 40th St. Bridge
to Millvale, St. Nicholas Church
with its Maxo Vanka murals,
religion brought into the real world
of torture, mining, greed and war.
Jean-Marc Chatelier, flat blue shop
on a faded street in the worn mill town,
thrifty, proud. The woman who sells me
fragrant croissants, chocolate cakes
with raspberry cream, tells me
she'd walked in her wedding dress to the church
just up the street, reception in the fire hall,
but her son wants limousines.

## Things Seen/Unseen

We took our dishes, vanilla ice cream
with fresh blueberries, to wash.

In the sink a baby mouse wearing gray velvet,
shivering whiskers, no clue how he'd come in.

There used to be holes from outside under the stove,
but a bamboo floor closed them off. Had we

left the front screen door ajar? But if so, how
did the mouse climb up to the counter-top,

fall into the steep-sided stainless steel sink? I cleaned
the cupboards overhead, prospecting for a nest

of mewing mice, protective mother, but no evidence,
though now the cupboard's clean and neatly organized.

Did the mouse come up through the drain? The basket
was in its usual place. No way that mouse could have

got into our kitchen, which is what
leads people to imagine God.

## The Logistics of Heaven

The hospice nurse told my daughter how lucky she was.
*You'll get to see my mother before I do,* was what she said.

I wondered how that would work. You go to Heaven,
walk in through Pearly Gates and straight away

spot the person you're looking for? An Internet query
tells me that give or take five billion, something like

100 billion people have lived on this earth since people
were distinct from other animals. So there's a problem

of logistics. Think of the Vietnam Memorial, its walls
that mirror you with names of the dead, so many

it takes a thick directory to find someone particular.
When I was a girl, a Mormon missionary trying

to convert my parents, asked my father, *Wouldn't you like
to think, Sir, that after your death you'd be married to this*

*fine woman for Time and Eternity?* My father grinned,
*Oh, I don't know. One lifetime might be enough.*

## Mend

The lovely wool sweater
hand-knit by a dear old friend

for my daughter's 36th birthday
twelve years ago. I wear it with

a cotton turtleneck so the wool
won't castigate my skin, put it on

the other night against the cold
and found that moths had eaten

a hole in the back. Washed it gently,
let it dry on the rack in the basement.

The friend who'd knit it searched
and found the wool she'd used and today

I darned the sweater with its mother wool,
the hole now invisible.

But when I wear it, I feel how short
the time was between Emily's

birthday and her death
less than a month later.

**It's like**


wearing
someone else's
mind, ill-fitting,
pockets in
the wrong places,
hem coming slightly
undone, as if I'd
picked up a stranger's
coat, have left
the building
wearing it and know,
as I feel the lining
against my arm,
that it's not mine
but I don't
have any other.

# Four

*The poet, tossing pebbles,*
*Muses on rings with rings.*
*—Carolyn Kizer, "Linked Verses"*

## In the Interest of Public Health

1.

When tight lacing into corsets
was in vogue, woman proved.
the weaker sex,
her organs squeezed, distorted

like her feet in six-inch heels,

the broken toes and arches
that made Chinese women
dainty cripples.

2.

*Hysteria* in women once caused,
by the *wandering womb*, excess of sex—
or lack thereof. Symptoms:
faintness, nerves, desire, insomnia, fluid retention,
heaviness in abdomen, muscle spasm, shortness of breath,
irritability, loss of appetite for food or sex, a tendency
to cause trouble.

The cure was pelvic massage—
electric vibrators were a hit
well before vacuum cleaners and electric irons
made it to the market.

3.

Nineteenth century doctor Samuel Cartwright
who practiced in Mississippi and Louisiana,
discovered a new infectious disease
whose symptom was slaves running away from masters.

Cartwright delivered a paper describing this illness
to the Louisiana Medical Association,
gave it a Greek name:
*drapetes*, runaway slave; *mania*, illness or derangement:
thus *drapetomania*.

His research had heft—the *Bible* told him so—
his work spread rapidly throughout southern states.
The cure was amputation of the toes.

4.

The way to end the epidemic
of death and injury by gunfire,
says the National Rifle Association,

is for more people to have more
and more powerful guns.

*Phalanxomania* we might call this fixation
from the Greek *phalanx* for soldiers that attack in close formation.

For *mania*, see above.

## Vile Things Precious

*—The art of our necessities is strange that can make vile
things precious. King Lear, III, 2*

I read myself to sleep on mayhem,
murder mysteries, the straight line—
crime to suspects through complications—
the world's ills set right.

Grizzleys catch salmon swimming
upstream to spawn and die,
excrete the salmony-nitrogen,
feeding nearby spruce.

Some countries still harvest whales
for food and research. And monster
container ships collide with the curious
behemoths, goliaths in asymmetrical battle.

Whales go down to feed in underwater
sea beds, surfacing to pee and poop
great log-sized turds at surface,
downwards drifting fertilizer for oceanic

gardens that feed schools of fish so there's
plenty to satisfy whales *and* fishermen.
It's like digging in compost, turning
up earthworms wriggling away from light,

small, helpful creatures digesting dirt
and rock, padding their burrows
with decaying leaves, making the soil
plants love.

## Black Man Walking

black man walking down the street—
black man sitting to wait for his kids from school—
black woman kissing her white boyfriend on a Hollywood street
    which cops take to be a reason to put her in handcuffs—
black man gasping *I can't breathe*—
black woman driving a red Nissan with her four children
    stopped because the cops are looking for a tan Toyota—
black teen-ager beaten by police who imagine
    he's up to no good when he cuts across the lawn
    to visit his grandmother,
    and the boy, a violist, is hurt enough
    that he can't
    play viola
    anymore.

One instance
    after another
    after another,
    another....

## Andrew Fouts Plays Emily's Violin

I hadn't thought the Rombauts violin
would sound so familiar in our long
front room, wood floors, high ceilings,

where Emily first played it for us,
taking it for a test run as she considered
whether we should buy it. But even

as another violinist fingered and bowed,
the sound fit like comfortable worn clothes
settling on our old bones.

## Losing Memory

It's the small things—
forgetting the name

at the tip
of my tongue

the flicking away
of the word I know—

rainbow trout
in the cold mountain stream

that flirts
with the world of oxygen.

## The Mole

on my flabby underarm
grew crusty.

The dermatologist took
it off with nitrogen

gave me a brochure
that said such things

were *barnacles of old age*
as if I were a pier

standing in salt water
or a whale

hung about
with merit badges.

## Acoustic


Today I washed
bathroom towels
the colors of
paprika and saffron
hung them out
on the backyard
line to dry
leaving
black and white tile
walls and floor
where everything
I say echoes
back to me

## Ten Ferraris, 2011

On *60 Minutes*—
homeless children,

kids who go
to school,

care for younger siblings,
do homework

in the public library,
use its computers,

live in their dad's old truck,
or in the car, on the street,

scrounge for food,
wash clothes and hair

in gas station
bathrooms,

hardly sleep,
afraid.

The *New York Times*
said on Thanksgiving

that Nieman Marcus
sold out

of Ferraris at $395,000 each
within 50 minutes

of making ten of them
available.

## City Birds

As I cross Murray and Forbes where a black butterfly
stands fluttering on a column of thick heat rising
almost visible from tarry pavement, a pair
of yellow warblers on the telephone wire
sings *sweet-sweet-sweet-a-sweet*. On my way
home, car stopped at Wightman and Wilkins,
I see a swift gray bird, beak trailing long grass,
streak into the P in *CVS Pharmacy,*
the P and a's shrill with fierce baby bird cries.

Last week as we left Harris's in Shadyside after dinner
with our kids and their kids, we joined a crowd across
the street watching a tiny hole in the brick, no more
than an inch across as a still tinier bird bulleted into it.
We peered through dusk into dark, glimpsed
minute beaks squawking open for the smallest
of split seconds before the mother crowded
the hatchlings out of sight of gawkers.

## A Cold in Summer

In summer you want
to throw the covers off
as you look out on
wilding gangs of weeds
and vines that replicate
and multiply.

## Driving home from Downtown after a long meeting

through the Strip, up Polish Hill, skirting Oakland,
past quiet Amberson's stately houses,
to the intersection with busy 5th Avenue,
east/west traffic surging homeward
into and away from setting sun.

At the green light, started to turn left.
Halfway into the intersection
I was hit broadside,
heard my own voice small, *Oh no!*
Stunned, needed to get out of the intersection,
U-turned back to where I'd been.
The other driver followed.
Levered myself over the emergency brake
and out the right-hand door.
The other driver, gray faced,
said he hadn't seen the red light.
Two students walking by called 911,
wrote names, phone numbers on the folder
I'd brought back from my meeting.
Hook & ladder, medics came, police.
We, strangers, intimate by accident, traded
information we'd both hoped never to need.

Drove home to my friendly red house
with its generous porch, lattice thick with white clematis,
shaken, sore. All I wanted was sleep
but had to answer questions, tell the tale,
to my insurance voice, then his.

Now, three days later, parts of my body
I hardly knew I had ache
and I want to sleep and sleep
but can't sleep.

## Laundry in Moonlight

Five loads of laundry after guests,
extra sheets and towels and napkins.

I let underpants and socks pile up
until we're down to the ones

with sprung elastic. It takes all morning,
into early afternoon before everything

is hung out on the line, not dry by dark.
I leave it up to breeze and moonlight.

## The World Should So Amaze Us

In the *New York Times* I learn
about the ordered existence of ants

who teach the little ones the way to food,
lead them along, pause while the youngsters

learn the route; ants who cure disease
by licking their sick ants,

which immunizes the licking ants.
The *Times* says that *Elephants rumble*

*to communicate, sending vibrations across*
*the landscape that other elephants can feel*

*through their feet*—low signals sent from far away.
Those heavy tree-trunk feet with spongy

cushions to absorb the pounding of such weight.
Elephants, noted for sharing, for nurturing

their young, re-visit the bones of their dead.
My friend saw sea turtles off the coast of Kauai,

said they seemed as curious about tourists
as *vice versa* and I've read that gray whales,

off the Pacific coast, nudge the boats, watch
the tourists who come to watch the whales.

## A list of things that give me pleasure


the sensuality of chopping onions, small resistance to the knife,
cooking the pearly chunks until they give up sugar
that caramelizes brown, perfuming the whole house;

the quiet clarity of hanging laundry out where I hear birdsong,
sheets, corners matched, jeans hung from hems, drying in air;
the small resurrection of darning socks with the wooden egg,

separating strands of thread to fit through the needle's eye,
making a weave that closes up the hole a toe or heel has made;
the liturgy of washing windows in spring, gray of winter dissolving

into hot water with vinegar while dirty water runs up my arms
and I finish with wadded newspaper so that I see the world new and clean;
the physicality of washing the Tibetan rugs, made of yak wool, spread

on the back yard flagstones where Dev gets down on his young knees,
rubs a bar of Ivory soap into the warp and weft we've soaked with the hose.
Scrubbing, rinsing, hefting the turnover, repeating on the topside

until they're too heavy to lift and Bob has to help us sling them
on the fence around the garbage pails and air conditioner, where they
drip dry for a couple of days, colors fresh on creamy background.

## Color

alight,
incandescent
after

a day of gray rain
the sun lights up
oriental poppies

next to purple
Siberian iris
and the colors

are stained glass
waving slightly
in the wind

## Blackpoll Warbler

*Not much bigger*
*than a hummingbird—*

weighs *as much as*
*a double-A battery.*

Scientists fit a tiny
geolocator to its leg,

track its migration
over 1,700 miles

in three days and nights
Small wonders seem,

somehow, holier
than all the miracles

religion preaches. It
first feasts on insects,

doubling its weight,
then flies non-stop

from New England
to South America.

**What I Didn't Expect—**


the way you can't understand how atoms
juggle everything solid
or how the sun's hot plasma
is woven with hydrogen and helium—
in the middle of the night
getting up to go to the bathroom
takes a moment's steadying,
that old is different from young,
that we still admire one another's aging bodies,
that my breasts sag, arms drape loose flesh,
that we lie in morning light, make love
to the sounds of birds, their separate lives,
the hush of snow.

## Pith and Moment

*...enterprises of great pith and moment*
*—Hamlet, Act III*

As I hang the first load of wash
on my new umbrella-folding clothesline
set in the 18-inch hole my son dug
among the hostas and spent spirea
in the back yard, where already cicadas
weave their late summer brocade,

I exult in the free sun and wind
lifting wet sheets and towels, socks,
underpants, shirts and jeans

that I fold down—dry—
into the laundry basket
at the end of a clear day.

**Perfect Mind**
> *I fear I am not in my perfect mind.*
> —*King Lear*

That centrifugal force of age,
being whirled towards a destination

of absence, of not existing, of never
having existed except as diminished

memory in others' minds. How odd
that Lear, his arrogance burned away,

his foolish judgments upended,
is wisest when his mind softens,

thaws, flows like water
and he knows his child.

## Sing, Goddess!

of Calypso who detains Odysseus as he heads
home after fighting Troy for a decade,
of Athena intervening to free him
and when he almost drowns,
Ino saves him.
When he washes ashore,
Nausica succors him.
Then Scylla and Charybdis,
gorgons,
the sexy Sirens
and the sorceress Circe.

When he finally makes it home—twenty years away
at war and wandering—
there's Penelope, who's run the kingdom,
held off the greedy suitors, raised their son alone.

Maybe Homer was a man—
men came to conquer, pillage,
put the reigning women down—
but what if Homer was a woman? generations
of old women telling of Achilles, Hector, Priam,
while goddesses lurk, riptide under the surface.

It's Mother Earth, *wide-bosomed*, says Hesiod,
*Not from me, but from my mother, comes the tale
of how earth and sky were once one form.*

## The Highway and the Night Sky


I write about night sky so dense that, though
adorned with stars—even when lights throb

along the highway, pollute that pure, deep dark—
you can feel what I once did, exalted

in the universe. You can remind me how it is
to be young, a pair of lovers; I can tell you how

the death of my youngest child still pulsates
through my veins. The highway never speaks

of starlight nor young love nor the shudder
when earth's whole crust collapses.

# Notes

p. 16—Tierra Rejada is the name of Monroe Everett's—my stepfather's—citrus, avocado, walnut ranch near the town of Moorpark, CA. It is now run by my brother-in-law, Richard Brecunier and his son Josh and is used primarily as the site for weddings and other private parties. It is still often the site of filming for scenes in movies.

p. 18— I was working on a novel about Mozart's mother, *Stitches in Air: A Novel About Mozart's Mother*, published by Smoke&Mirrors Press, 2001.

p. 24—*A Field Book of the Stars* by William Tyler Olcott, G.P. Putnam's Sons,1907.

p. 34—*Wit*, a play by Margaret Edson, won the 1999 Pulitzer Prize for drama.

p. 50—You can hear the recorded music played on a natural horn by the trumpeter of Krakow at http://www.krakow-info.com/hejnal.htm. It breaks off at just the point when the actual trumpeter was shot in the throat by a Tatar arrow.

p. 76—*Evolution News and Views*, April 7, 2015.

Liane Ellison Norman's *Breathing the West: Great Basin Poems,* was published by Bottom Dog Press in the fall of 2012, a year in which a chapbook, *Driving Near the Old Federal Arsenal,* was released by Finishing Line Press and *Roundtrip* by Yesterdays Parties Press. Garrison Keillor read one of *Breathing the West's* poems, "Tree," on The Writer's Almanac, December 2, 2012. Norman has published individual poems in the *North American Review, Kestrel, The Fourth River, 5 AM, Grasslimb, Rune, Hot Metal Press, The Pittsburgh Post Gazette, Pittsburgh City Paper, The New People, Speaking for Myself* (an anthology published by Chicory Blue Press), *The Platte Valley Review, ruthh.wordpress.com, Squirrel Hill Magazine* and in *Voices From the Attic* and *Come Together: Imagine Peace* anthologies. She won the Wisteria Prize for poetry in 2006 from Paper Journey Press and has published two earlier books of poetry, *The Duration of Grief and Keep;* a book about nonviolent protest against nuclear bomb parts makers, *Mere Citizens: United, Civil and Disobedient,* a biography, *Hammer of Justice: Molly Rush* and the *Plowshares Eight,* upon which Tammy Ryan's play, *Molly's Hammer,* is based; a novel, *Stitches in Air: A Novel About Mozart's Mother,* and many articles, essays and reviews.

CPSIA information can be obtained
at www.ICGtesting.com
Printed in the USA
BVOW06s0046140117
473504BV00004B/17/P

9 781635 340945